Drawing and Learning About Monster Trucks

Using Shapes and Lines

written and illustrated by
Amy Bailey Muehlenhardt

Thanks to our advisers for their expertise, research, and advice:

Linda Frichtel, Design Adjunct Faculty, MCAD
Minneapolis, Minnesota

Susan Kesselring, M.A., Literacy Educator
Rosemount–Apple Valley–Eagan (Minnesota) School District

Amy Bailey Muehlenhardt
grew up in Fergus Falls, Minnesota, and attended Minnesota State University in Moorhead. She holds a Bachelor of Science degree in Graphic Design and Art Education. Before coming to Picture Window Books, Amy was an elementary art teacher. She always impressed upon her students that "everyone is an artist." Amy lives in Mankato, Minnesota, with her husband, Brad, and daughter, Elise.

For Elise Lauren, my new smile.
ABM

Editorial Director: Carol Jones
Managing Editor: Catherine Neitge
Creative Director: Keith Griffin
Editor: Jill Kalz
Editorial Adviser: Bob Temple
Story Consultant: Terry Flaherty
Designer: Jaime Martens
Page Production: Picture Window Books
The illustrations in this book were created with pencil and colored pencil.

Picture Window Books
151 Good Counsel Drive
P.O. Box 669
Mankato, MN 56002-0669
1-877-845-8392
www.picturewindowbooks.com

Printed in the United States of America.

All books published by Picture Window Books are manufactured with paper containing at least 10 percent post-consumer waste.

Library of Congress Cataloging-in-Publication Data
Muehlenhardt, Amy Bailey, 1974–
Drawing and learning about monster trucks / written and illustrated by Amy Bailey Muehlenhardt.
p. cm. — (Sketch it!)
Includes bibliographical references and index.
ISBN 1-4048-1194-X (hardcover)
1. Trucks in art—Juvenile literature. 2. Monsters in art—Juvenile literature. 3. Drawing—Technique—Juvenile literature. I. Title: Monster trucks. II. Title.
NC825.T76M84 2005
743'.89629224—dc22 2005007176

Table of Contents

Everyone Is an Artist

There is no right or wrong way to draw!

With a little patience and some practice, anyone can learn to draw. Did you know every picture begins as a simple shape? If you can draw shapes, you can draw anything.

The Basics of Drawing

line—a long mark made by a pen, a pencil, or another tool

guideline—a line used to help you draw; the guideline will be erased when your drawing is almost complete

shade—to color in with your pencil

value—the lightness or darkness of an object

shape—the form or outline of an object or figure

diagonal—a shape or line that leans to the side

Before you begin, you will need:

a pencil,
an eraser,
lots of paper!

Four Tips for Drawing

1. Draw very lightly.
   Try drawing light, medium, and dark lines. The softer you press, the lighter the lines will be.
2. Draw your shapes.
   When you are finished drawing, connect your shapes with a sketch line.
3. Add details.
   Details are small things that make a good picture even better.
4. Color your art.
   Use your colored pencils, crayons, or markers to create backgrounds.

Let's get started!

Simple shapes help you draw.

Practice drawing these shapes before you begin.

circle

A circle is round like a ball.

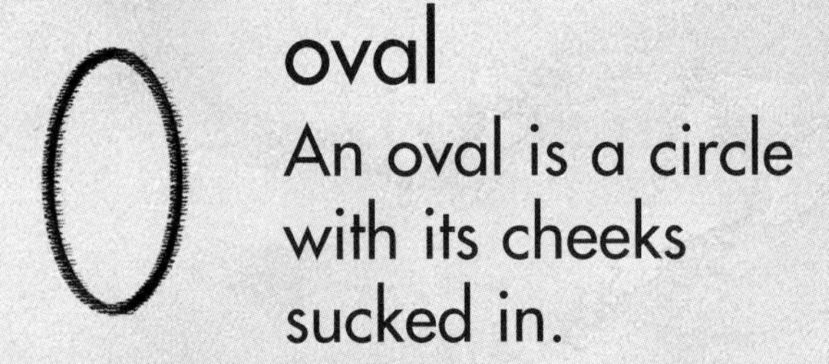

oval

An oval is a circle with its cheeks sucked in.

arc

An arc is half of a circle. It looks like a turtle's shell.

square

A square has four equal sides and four corners.

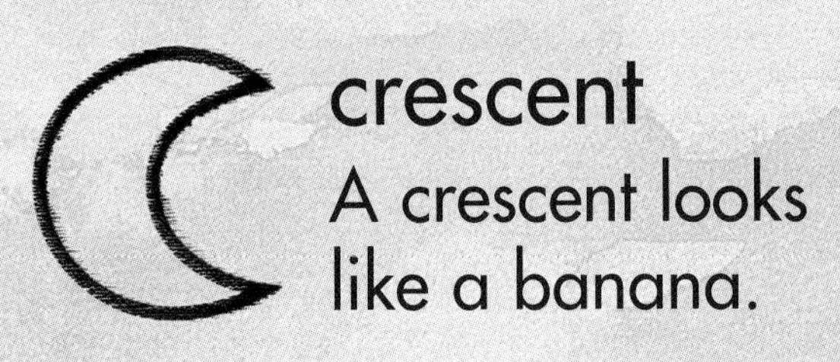

crescent

A crescent looks like a banana.

triangle

A triangle has three sides and three corners.

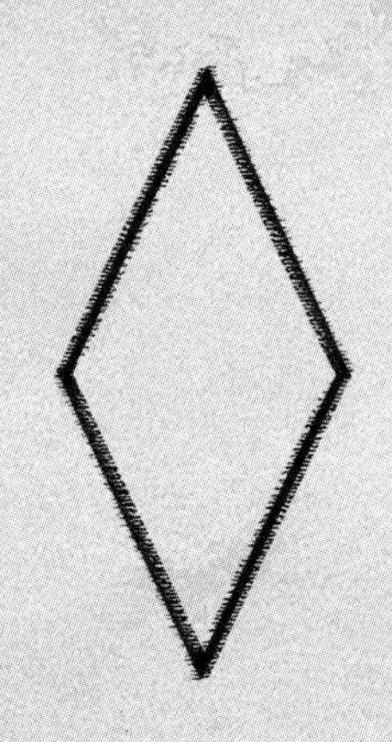

diamond

A diamond is two triangles put together.

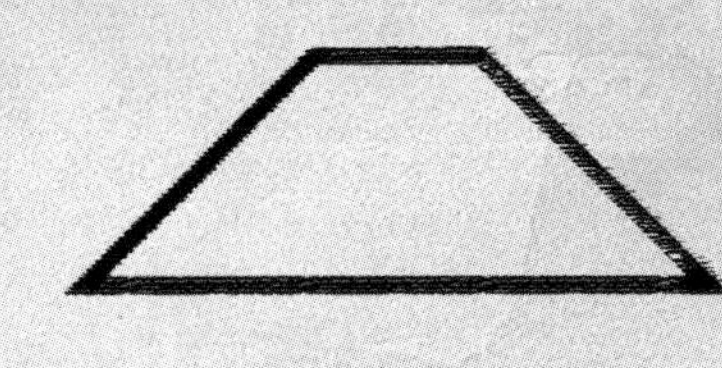

trapezoid

A trapezoid has four sides and four corners. Two of its sides are different lengths.

rectangle

A rectangle has two long sides, two short sides, and four corners.

You will also use lines when drawing.

Practice drawing these lines.

vertical

A vertical line stands tall like a tree.

horizontal

A horizontal line lies down and takes a nap.

diagonal

A diagonal line leans to the side.

dizzy

A dizzy line spins around and around.

zigzag

A zigzag line is sharp and pointy.

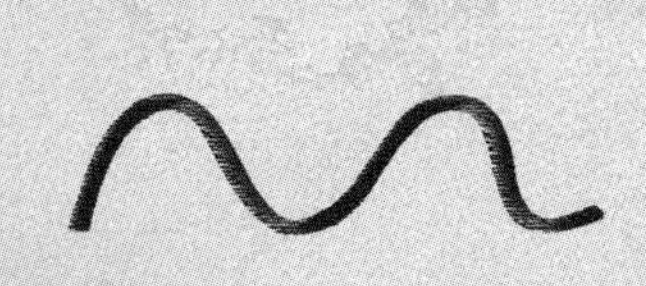

wavy

A wavy line moves up and down like a roller coaster.

Remember to practice drawing.

While using this book, you may want to stop drawing at step five or six. That's great! Everyone is at a different drawing level.

Don't worry if your picture isn't perfect. The important thing is to have fun.

Be creative!

Nasty Beast

Like most monster trucks, Nasty Beast is a pickup body propped up on huge knobby tires. Nasty Beast rolls over smaller cars, crushing them as it bounces along to the roar of the crowd.

Step 1

Draw two squares and two rectangles for the body.

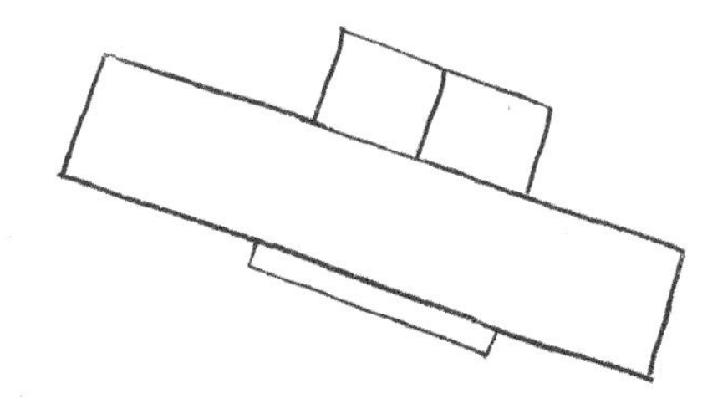

Step 2

Draw a square for the side window. Draw three diagonal lines for the front window. Add two arcs for the wheel wells.

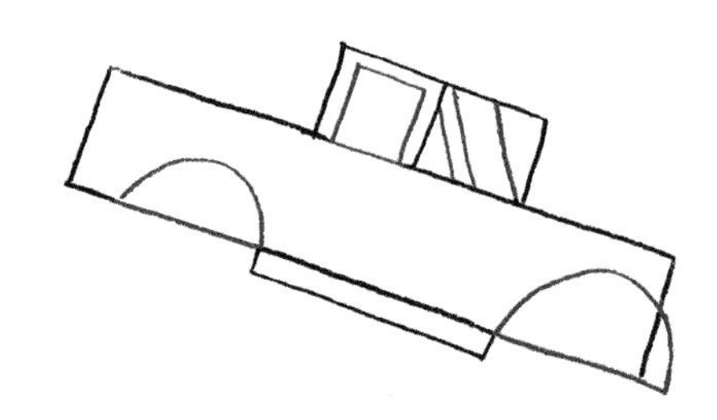

Step 3

Draw a rectangle for the back bumper and an arc for the front bumper.

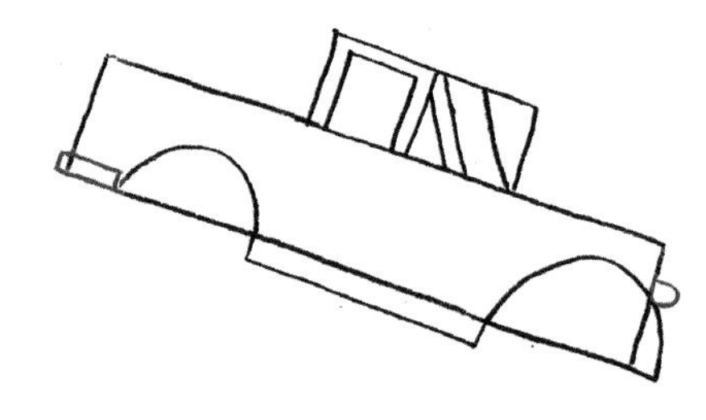

Step 4

Draw two more diagonal lines for the front window. Draw two circles for the tires. Add four circles for the hubcaps.

Step 5

Define the truck with a sketch line. Draw two curved lines for the door. Add a rectangle for the handle. Define the tires with wavy lines.

Step 6

Erase the extra lines. Add details such as zigzag lines for the teeth, an eye and arm with claws on the side, and an axle.

Step 7

Color your truck and add a background.

Colonel Crusher

Colonel Crusher has the body of a wood-paneled station wagon. But this is no family car! Its owner, a former U.S. Army colonel, gave the vehicle a very patriotic paint job.

Step 1

Draw a rectangle and a trapezoid for the body.

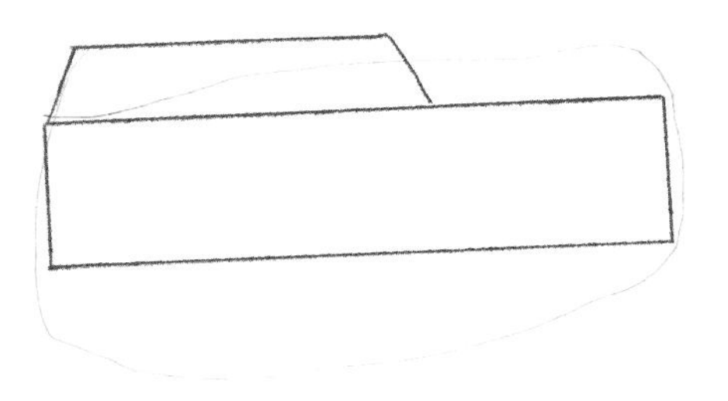

Step 2

Draw two arcs for the wheel wells. Draw a diagonal and vertical line for the windows.

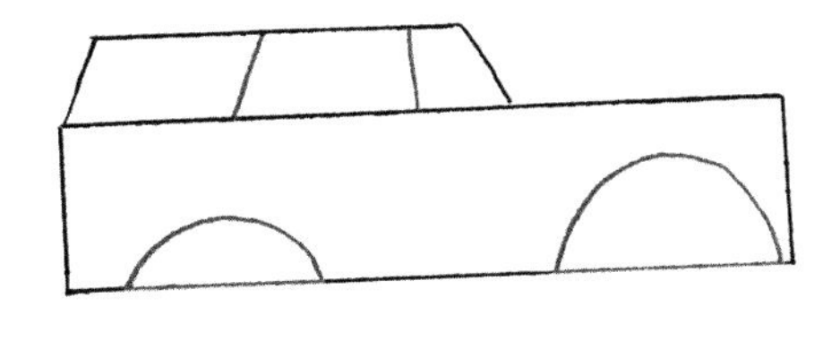

Step 3

Draw two circles for the tires. Add four circles for the hubcaps.

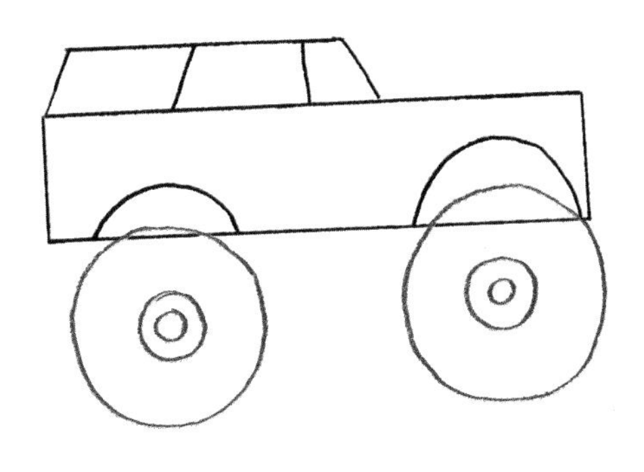

Step 4

Draw a large rectangle for the wood-paneled side. Add two rectangles for the bumpers.

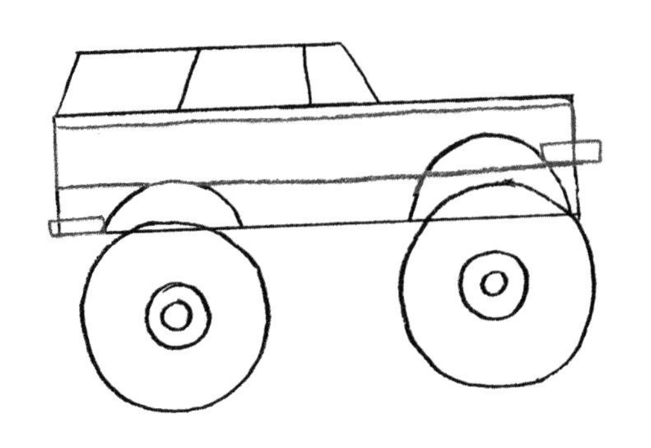

Step 5

Define the truck with a sketch line. Add a rectangle for the axle. Define the tires with wavy lines.

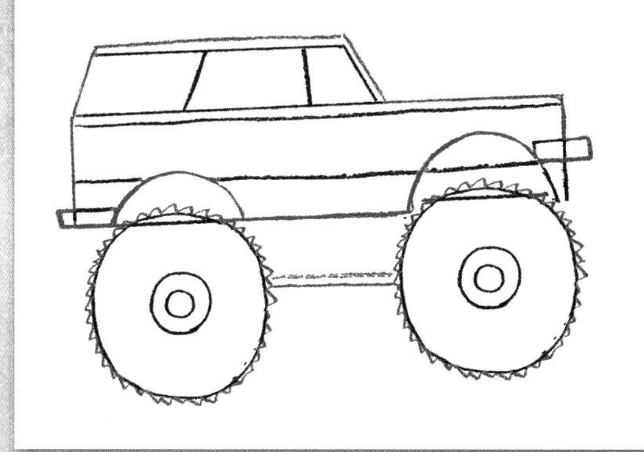

Step 6

Erase the extra lines. Add details such as stars, stripes, and an eagle on the side.

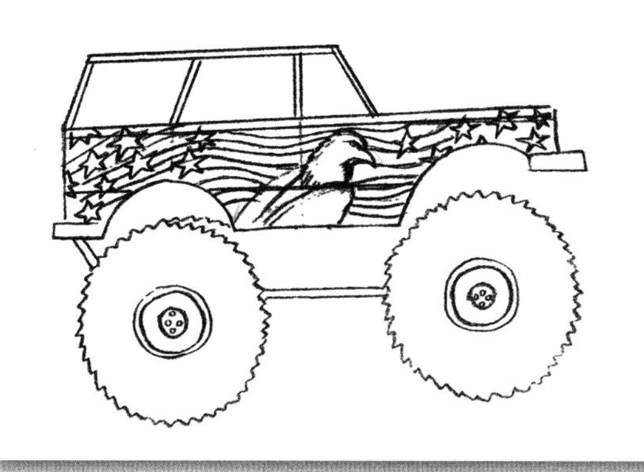

Step 7

Color your truck and add a background.

9-1-1

The 9-1-1 monster truck has the body of an ambulance and some of the biggest tires around. The numbers "9-1-1" are painted in red on each side. If you need help, this is the truck to call!

Step 1

Draw a rectangle and a square for the body. Add a slender triangle for the roof. Draw a rectangle for the bottom of the truck.

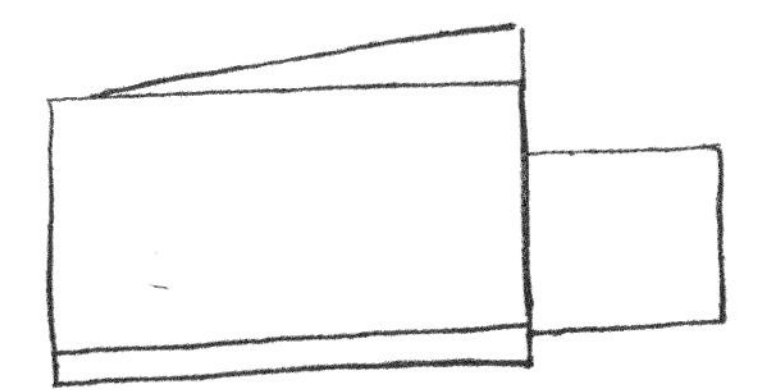

Step 2

Draw two arcs for the wheel wells. Draw a square for the window. Add two squares for the bumpers.

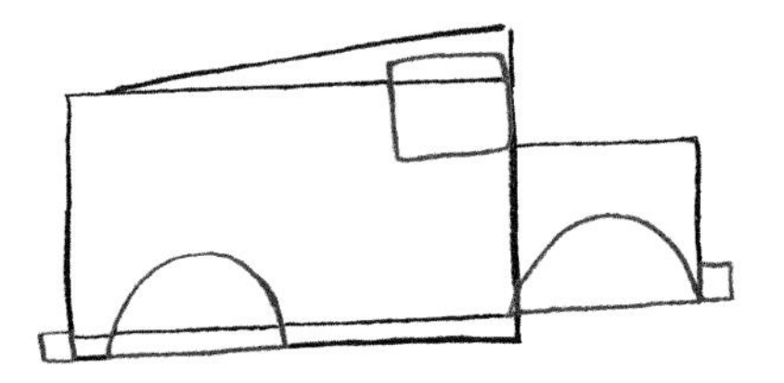

Step 3

Draw two diagonal lines for the front window. Draw a trapezoid for the siren. Add an oval for the headlight.

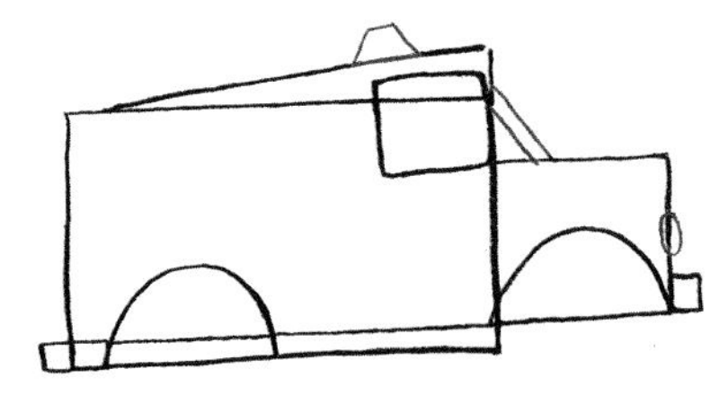

Step 4

Draw two circles for the tires. Add four circles for the hubcaps. Add a rectangle for the axle.

Step 5

Define the truck with a sketch line. Draw a diagonal line for the door. Define the tires with wavy lines.

Step 6

Erase the extra lines. Add details such as the numbers "9-1-1" and curved lines on the side.

Step 7

Color your truck and add a background.

Tidal Wave

Tidal Wave has a sharp, racing look to it. White and gold waves splash across its bright blue hood and wash down the truck's sides. Even the headlight covers are blue-tinted.

Step 1

Draw a trapezoid for the hood and a rectangle for the grill of the truck.

Step 2

Draw a horizontal line across the middle of the rectangle. Draw two trapezoids for the windshield.

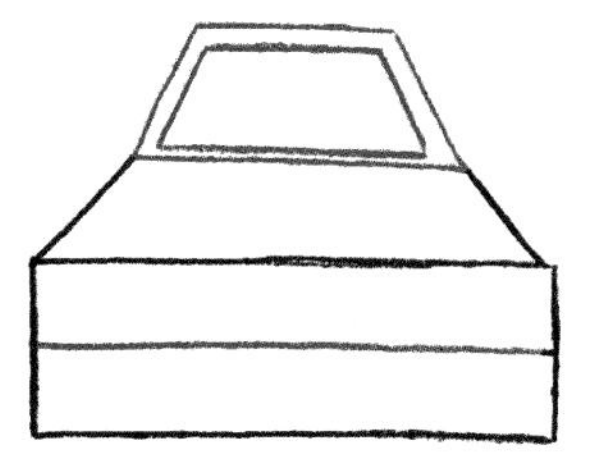

Step 3

Draw four circles for the lights. Draw two rectangles for the tires.

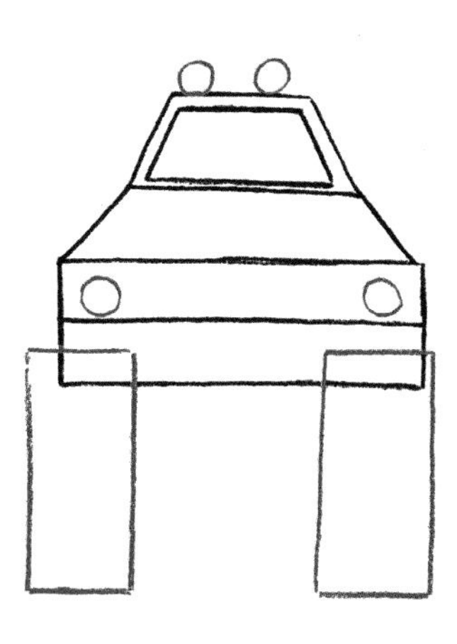

Step 4

Draw a rectangle and two diagonal lines for the axle.

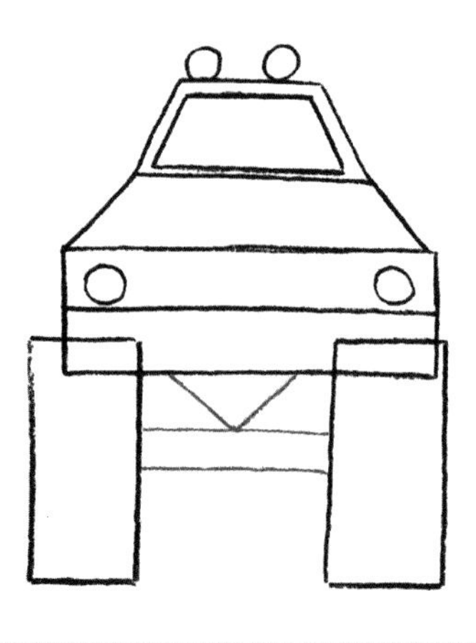

Step 5

Define the truck with a sketch line. Add a rectangle for the bumper. Define the tires with wavy lines.

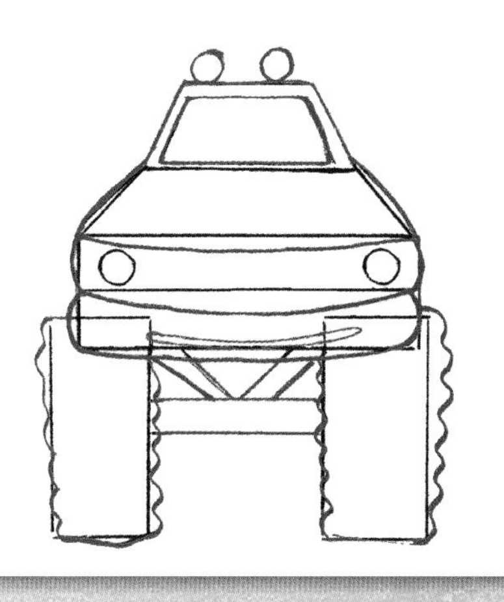

Step 6

Erase the extra lines. Add details such as tire treads, horizontal lines for the grill, and a wave on the hood.

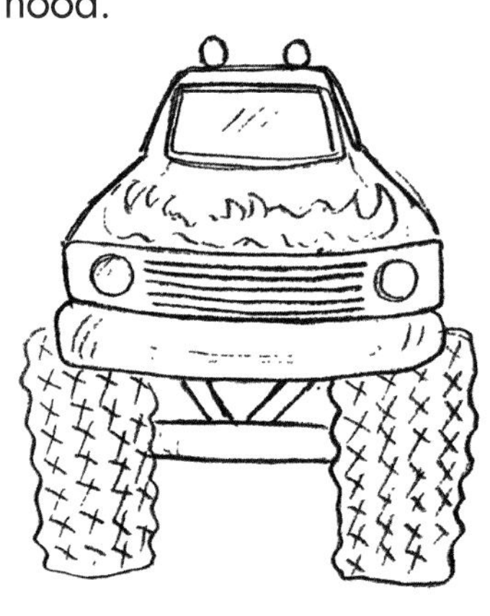

Step 7

Color your truck and add a background.

Rigormortis

Rigormortis is one of the most feared monster trucks of all. Its black paint job is highlighted with green flames. A graveyard scene, with ghosts and headstones, covers each side of this scary monster hearse.

Step 1

Draw two rectangles for the body.

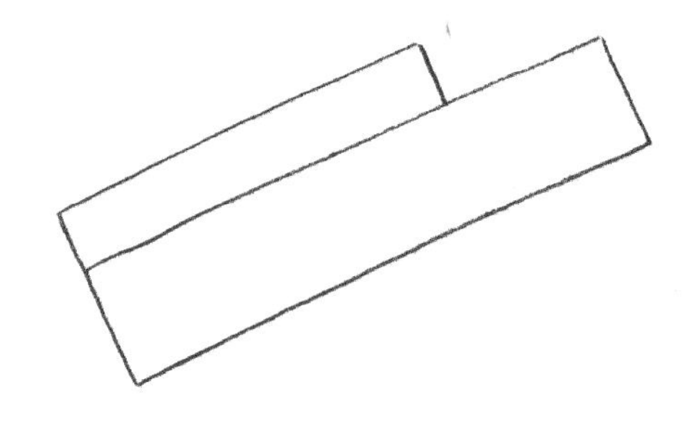

Step 2

Draw a diagonal line for the door.
Draw two arcs for the wheel wells.

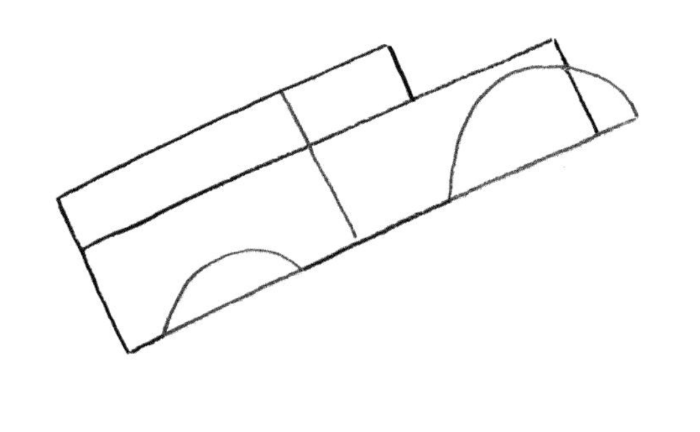

Step 3

Draw an oval for the headlight.
Add one rectangle for the back bumper and another for the front bumper.

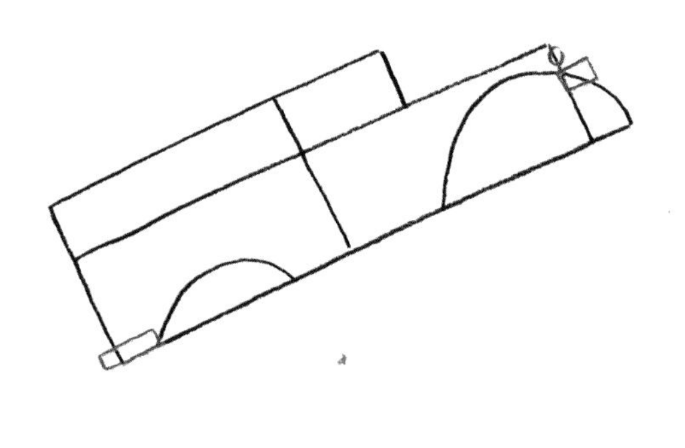

Step 4

Draw two circles for the tires.
Add four circles for the hubcaps.
Draw a rectangle for the window.

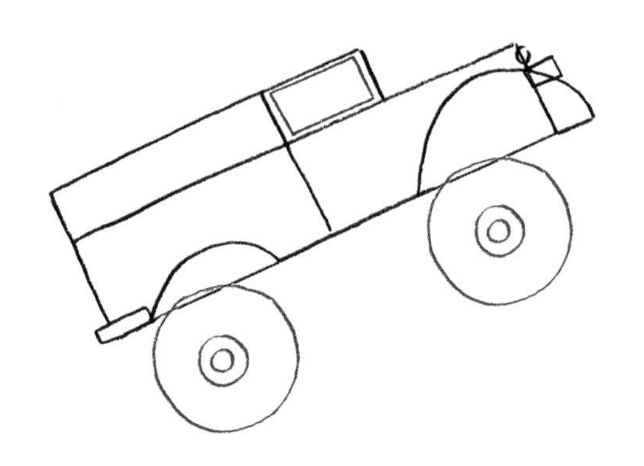

Step 5

Define the truck with a sketch line. Add two curved lines to shape the window. Define the tires with wavy lines.

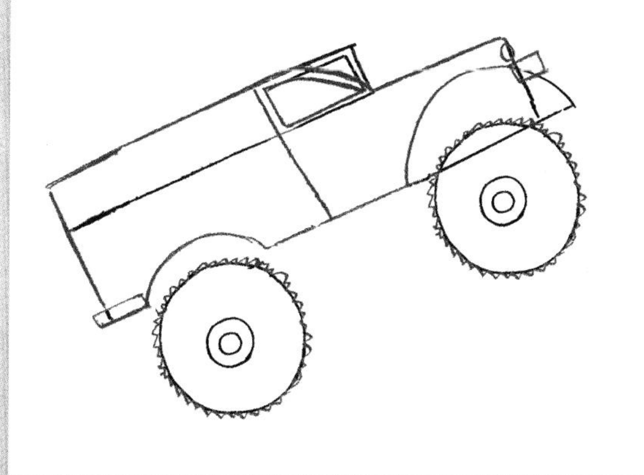

Step 6

Erase the extra lines. Draw a rectangle for the axle. Add details such as a ghost, headstones, and zigzag flames on the side.

Step 7

Color your truck and add a background.

High Explosives

One of the most brightly colored monster trucks is High Explosives. It has white stars on a background of yellow, orange, red, and blue. The words "High Explosives" light up both sides.

Step 1

Draw two rectangles and two squares for the body.

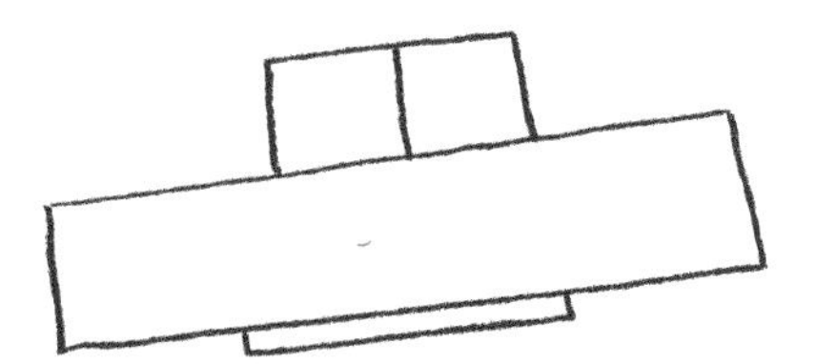

Step 2

Draw a square inside one square. Draw two diagonal lines inside the other square. Draw four arcs for the wheel wells.

Step 3

Draw two diagonal lines for the window. Draw two circles for the tires. Add two circles for the hubcaps.

Step 4

Draw two arcs for the bumpers. Draw a rectangle for the axle. Add two stars to the hubcaps.

Step 5

Finish the side window with one diagonal line. Add two curved lines for the door. Define the truck with a sketch line. Define the tires with wavy lines.

Step 6

Erase the extra lines. Add details such as dizzy lines, zigzag lines, and the words "High Explosives" on the side.

Step 7

Color your truck and add a background.

Bad Voodoo

Bad Voodoo sports crocodile teeth on its grill and sharp claws on its fenders. This monster sedan might just take a bite out of cars instead of crushing them!

Step 1

Draw three arcs for the front of the truck.

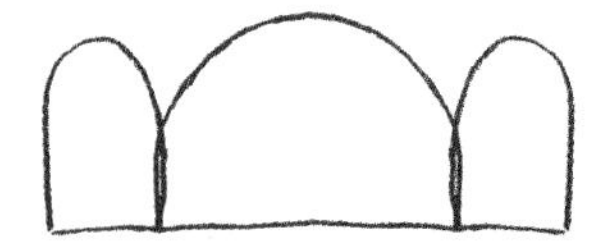

Step 2

Draw an arc for the roof and a trapezoid for the windshield.

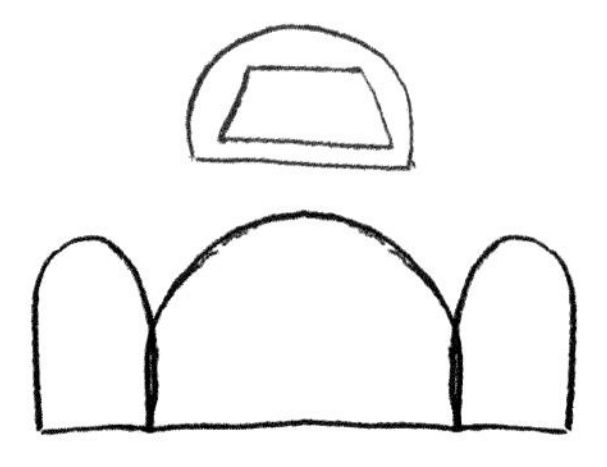

Step 3

Connect the roof to the front of the truck with two diagonal lines. Add two circles for the headlights.

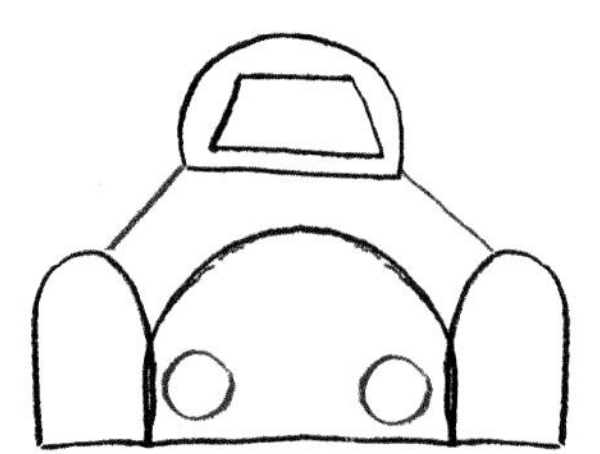

Step 4

Draw two rectangles for the tires. Add another rectangle for the axle.

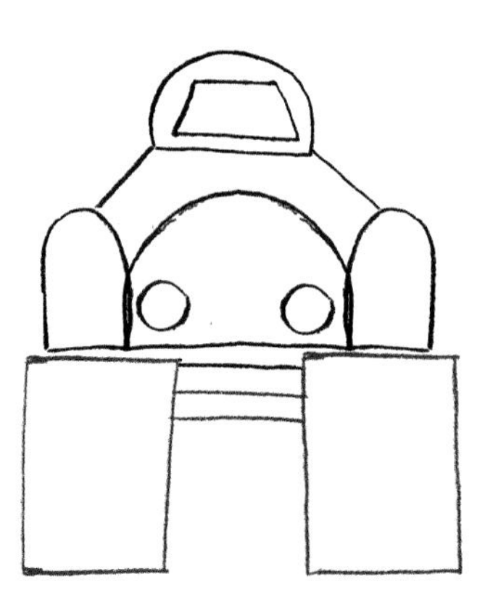

Step 5

Draw a rectangle for the bumper. Define the truck with a sketch line. Define the tires with wavy lines.

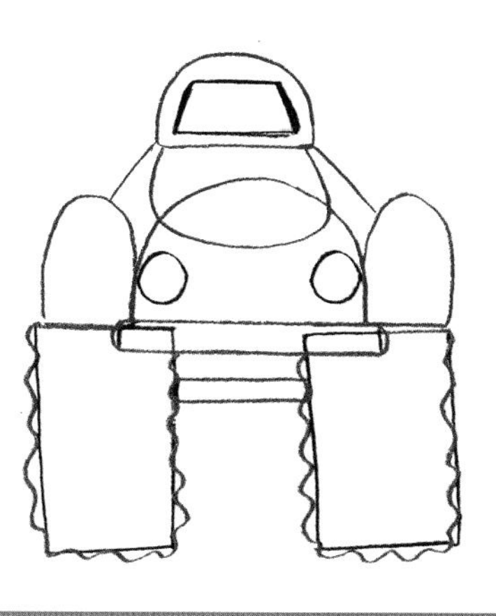

Step 6

Erase the extra lines. Add details such as tire treads, eyes, nostrils, and zigzag teeth and claws.

Step 7

Color your truck and add a background.

Tarantula

If you're afraid of spiders, this isn't the monster truck for you. Tarantula sports an all-black paint job—even the rims are black. Across the sides and hood is a neon orange spider web.

Step 1

Draw three rectangles for the front and rear of the truck. Draw two circles for the headlights.

Step 2

Connect the front and back rectangles with four diagonal lines. You are creating a three-dimensional box. Draw two arcs for the wheel wells.

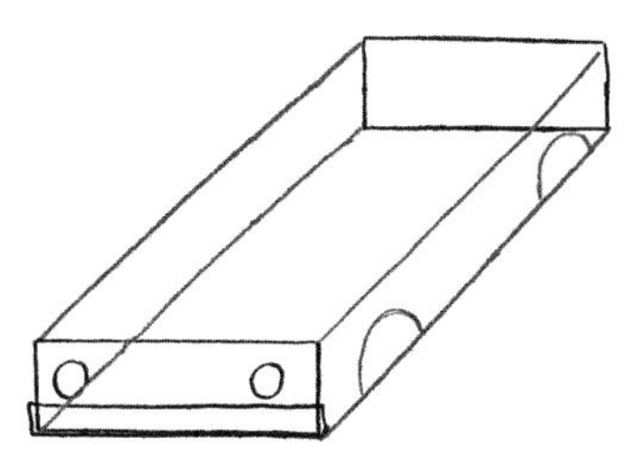

Step 3

Draw two rectangles for the windows. Draw three ovals and three curved lines for the tires. Add three ovals for the hubcaps.

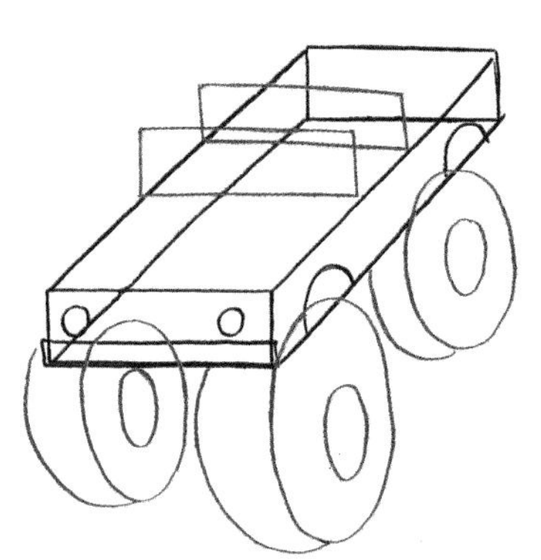

Step 4

Connect the front and back rectangles with two diagonal lines. Add a square for the side window and a rectangle for the windshield.

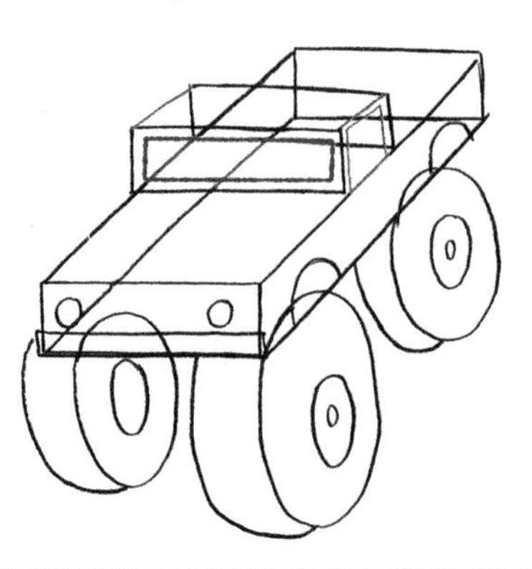

Step 5

Draw two diagonal lines for the door. Draw two horizontal lines for the axle. Define the truck with a sketch line. Define the tires with wavy lines.

Step 6

Erase the extra lines. Add details such as a grill, a door handle, and a spider in a web on the hood.

Step 7

Color your truck and add a background.

To Learn More

More Books to Read

Doeden, Matt. *Monster Trucks.* Mankato, Minn.: Capstone Press, 2004.

Griffin, Georgene. *Monster Trucks.* Vero Beach, Fla.: Rourke Publishing, 2001.

Hart, Christopher. *How to Draw Sports Cars, Monster Trucks, & Fighter Jets.* New York: Watson–Guptill Publications, 2000.

Levete, Sarah. *Monster Trucks.* Chicago: Raintree Publishing, 2005

On the Web

FactHound offers a safe, fun way to find Web sites related to topics in this book.

All of the sites on FactHound have been researched by our staff.

1. Visit *www.facthound.com*
2. Type in this special code: 140481194X
3. Click on the FETCH IT button.

Your trusty FactHound will fetch the best sites for you!

Look for all the books in the Sketch It! series:

Drawing and Learning About ...

Bugs
Cars
Cats
Dinosaurs
Dogs
Faces
Fashion
Fish
Horses
Jungle Animals
Monsters
Monster Trucks